T
MARRIAGE IN ME

A. Faye Bell

Before You Say, "I Do"

THERE'S A MARRIAGE IN ME
A. Faye Bell

All rights reserved. No portion of this book may be reproduced, scanned, stored in a retrieval system, transmitted in any form or by any means – electronically, mechanically, photocopy, recording or any other – except for brief quotations in printed reviews, without the written permission of the publisher. Please do not participate in or encourage piracy of copyrighted materials in violation of the author's rights. Purchase on authorized editions.

Copy and Content Editing
Anthony KaDarrell Thigpen
of Literacy in Motion

Library of Congress Cataloging-in-Publication Data
ISBN: 979-8-9881580-1-1

B. Faye Bell
THERE'S A MARRIAGE IN ME
Before You Say, "I Do"

Christian / Self-Help
Printed in the United States of America

Dedication

There's A Wife in Me
I dedicate this book to my mom, Gwendolyn. She was a remarkable woman and a wonderful wife to my dad. She taught me what a caring, loving, patient, and loyal wife looks like.

I acknowledge both of my grandmothers, Frances Setzer and Clemus Lomick. I was blessed to grow up (be raised) with two of the strongest, smartest, loving, and God-fearing women.

And to my husband and best friend, Shawn, I am blessed to be covered, loved, and inspired by you. Not only do I love you, but I respect, honor, and adore you.

THERE'S A MARRIAGE IN ME

TABLE OF CONTENT

Introduction
PREPARING FOR MY FUTURE   **pg. 6**

Chapter 1
WHAT IS MARRIAGE ABOUT
More than a Fairytale   **pg. 15**

Chapter 2
WIVES TO BE
Embodying the Lifestyle of a Helpmate   **pg. 35**

Chapter 3
THE HATS HUSBANDS WEAR
The Interchanging Duties of a Spouse   **pg. 45**

Chapter 4
PREPARING FOR MARRIAGE
Steps to Take Prior to Meeting the One.   **pg. 55**

Chapter 5
RESTORING THE TEMPLE
Wholeness of Body, Soul, and Spirit   **pg. 74**

Index
Q&A SESSION
Singles Seminar 2023   **pg. 82**

About the Author
MOTIVATIONAL SPEAKER
Creating a Culture of Healthy Marriages   **pg.102**

Introduction

Preparing for My Future

Deciding to get married is one of the most critical decisions in life. It's a commitment that involves a lot of spiritual, emotional, social, and financial investment. However, making the right decision can lead to a fulfilling and happy life, while making the wrong decision can cause stress and heartbreak. This book, "There's a Marriage in Me" will discuss the key factors to consider when deciding whether to get married.

Internal Factors

1. Compatibility: Are you and your partner compatible regarding values, goals, and interests?
2. Commitment: Are you both committed to making the relationship work?
3. Communication: Can you communicate effectively with each other and resolve conflicts?
4. Trust: Do you trust each other and feel secure in the relationship?
5. Emotional maturity: Are you and your partner emotionally mature enough to handle the ups and downs of marriage?
6. Personal Readiness: Are you personally ready for marriage? Do you feel emotionally and mentally prepared?

External Factors

1. Support from family and friends: Are your families and friends supportive of your relationship?
2. Social and cultural factors: Do you share similar social and cultural backgrounds? Are there any cultural or social barriers that might impact your relationship?
3. Financial factors: Are you both financially stable? Do you have a plan for managing your finances as a couple?
4. Career goals: Do you have similar career goals? Will your career paths allow for a stable and fulfilling marriage?
5. Health factors: Are you and your partner healthy? Are there any health issues that might impact your marriage?
6. Timing: Is this the right time for you to get married? Are there any external factors, such as a job or educational opportunities, that might impact your decision?

Over 90% of engaged couples spend more money and time investing on their wedding day than investing and preparing for their marriage. While two people are in love and have made their choice for a spouse, there is so much that I find out they don't know before entering a marriage. The first is the quality of their relationship skills and learning the right skills to have a difficult conversation. They often have disagreements or difficult conversations despite their love for each other. Many men and women don't know the right questions to ask, how to listen, and how to speak, so there is little reactivity in their dialogues. Another critical issue is that many individuals don't know how to discuss their own and the other person's history by asking the right questions to decide for their future. This is why finding a seasoned and experienced therapist to facilitate the critical issues before their wedding in the sessions. Good premarital counseling takes at least nine months of weekly therapy focusing on the essential points as they prepare for their future.

"There's a Marriage in Me" will help couples get to know each other better to settle down the right way. The answers to premarital questions can reveal more about your soon-to-be life partner. They can help to manage expectations. Premarital questions lead to clarity. Clarity leads to trust. If you are about to tie the knot, gentle reader, consider discussing some of the premarital questions we share below.

Marriage is beautiful and a natural longing. However, the reality is that love and the desire for it are not all and only issues in marriage. Marriage can be complex and challenging. It requires skills and well-informed discussions before entering and saying, "I Do." I have met with numerous couples who are dating or engaged who are stuck for a long time and don't know how to get unstuck, and the only thing that keeps them in is that "but I love her, or I love him," and that is how they enter marriage without proper vetting. Good premarital counseling can save your life and your marriage. Think of premarital questions as risk assessments. It helps to foresee areas of difficulty so you can confront them now or make plans for addressing them.

We want to make things easier for you. Therefore, we have categorized the questions into the five most critical premarital topics. So, get comfortable and ready to learn more about your soon-to-be marital partner. Quality lasting relationships start with good decision-making processes.

Decision-Making Process

1. Take your time: Don't rush into a decision. Take the time to think about your options and discuss them with your partner.
2. Seek advice: Talk to trusted family members and friends who have experience with marriage. Seek advice from a therapist or counselor if necessary.
3. Consider the future: Think about how your decision will impact your future. Will it lead to a happy and fulfilling life?
4. Listen to your intuition: Pay attention to your gut feeling. If something doesn't feel right, listening to your instinct is essential.
5. Be honest with yourself: Be honest about your feelings and concerns. Pay attention to red flags or warning signs.
6. Make a pro-con list: Write down the pros and cons of getting married. This can help you weigh your options and make an informed decision.

Deciding to get married is a big decision, and it's essential to consider all the factors involved. By evaluating your compatibility, commitment, communication, and other factors, you can make an informed decision that leads to a happy and fulfilling life. Remember to seek advice, and wise counsel, listen to your intuition, pray, and be honest with yourself throughout the decision-making process.

Making the decision that you are ready for marriage is personal and complex. Some additional factors to consider are your emotional and spiritual readiness. Readiness for commitment requires shared values and goals. It also demands the ability and willingness to communicate and resolve conflicts effectively. In addition, having open and honest conversations with your partner will be helpful and necessary. Finally, remember you must seek advice from trusted, like-minded individuals and premarital counseling from a licensed professional or an experienced pastor. Be sure your decision is guided by someone who cares about your future as God does. Afterward, only you can determine if you are ready for marriage.

Marriage plays a significant role in preparing for your future in many ways. Here are some of the ways marriage can impact your future planning:

1. Financial Planning: Marriage is a crucial aspect of financial planning as it involves sharing income, expenses, and assets. After marriage, couples

often combine their finances and make joint financial decisions. This includes creating a budget, saving for the future, and planning for retirement.

2. Career Planning: Marriage can impact career planning as it involves balancing work and personal life. Couples may need to make career decisions based on their spouse's job or family responsibilities. They may need to relocate or make other career changes aligning with their partner's goals.

3. Family Planning: Marriage is often seen as the first step towards starting a family. Couples may need to plan for the arrival of children, including the timing, childcare, and financial aspects. It's important to discuss family planning goals and expectations with your partner before getting married.

4. Personal Growth: Marriage can be an opportunity for personal growth and development. Couples may learn to navigate conflicts, communicate better, and compromise to make the relationship work. Marriage can provide a supportive environment for personal growth and self-improvement.

5. Legal and Social Benefits: Marriage provides legal and social benefits, such as tax benefits, inheritance rights, and access to health insurance. These benefits can impact your future planning, including financial, health, and estate planning.

Marriage plays a significant role in preparing for your future. It impacts financial planning, career planning, family planning, and personal growth and provides legal and social benefits. Therefore, discussing your goals, expectations, and concerns with your partner before getting married is essential for working together to plan for your future.

This book is a brilliant guide highlighting essential subject matter and bullet points to help readers process comprehensive information step-by-step. It has all the key components to help men and women prepare for their future. "There is a Marriage in Me" is written with singles in mind who have a deep desire to experience a lifetime of holy matrimony.

Chapter 1

WHAT IS MARRIAGE ABOUT
More than a Fairytale

Marriage is an important institution that has been celebrated and cherished for centuries. It is a sacred bond between two individuals who have decided to commit themselves to each other for life. Marriage provides a foundation for building a family and a future together. Traditionally, a healthy partnership between a husband and wife requires mutual respect, communication, and compromise.

Before getting married, each couple should understand what they are getting into. Marriage is a serious commitment that involves both emotional and legal responsibilities. Therefore, couples need to clearly know what they are committing to and the expectations that come with it.

Marriage requires deeply understanding each other's values, beliefs, and goals. It requires a willingness to work together to overcome challenges and to support each other through the ups and downs of life. Marriage is a partnership that involves both love and practical considerations such as finances, household responsibilities, and decision-making.

When couples enter marriage with a clear understanding of what they are getting into, they are better equipped to build a strong, healthy, and fulfilling relationship. They understand the importance of open communication, trust, and mutual support. As a result, they can navigate the challenges of marriage with greater resilience and are more likely to experience a lifetime of love and happiness.

In conclusion, marriage is an important institution that provides a foundation for building a family and a future together. Each couple should understand what they are getting into and be committed to working together to build a strong, healthy, and fulfilling relationship. Couples can create a lifetime of happiness and joy with love, respect, and willingness to work together. The first step toward entering a healthy relationship starts with this confession: "There is a Marriage in Me."

Marriage is a legally recognized union between two people, often involving a ceremony and social or religious traditions, in which they commit to sharing their lives as partners.

People may desire to be married for various reasons, most healthy marriages centered around key aspects, such as:

1. LOVE

Love is a complex and multi-faceted emotion that can be difficult to define. At its core, love involves a deep affection and attachment towards someone or something. Love can be romantic, platonic, familial, or even extend to non-human things like pets or hobbies. Here are some common aspects of love:

- Emotion: Love is an emotional experience that can bring joy, happiness, and fulfillment.
- Connection: Love involves a sense of connection and intimacy with someone or something. It can be a feeling of oneness or a sense of being at home with someone.
- Care: Love involves caring for someone or something deeply, including their happiness, well-being, and needs.
- Sacrifice: Love often involves sacrifice, whether it's giving up something you love for the other person's sake or putting their needs before your own.
- Acceptance: Love involves accepting someone or something for who they are, including their strengths and weaknesses.

- Commitment: Love often involves a commitment to the person or thing you love, including a willingness to work through challenges and obstacles together.

Love is a complex and multi-faceted emotion that involves deep affection, connection, care, sacrifice, acceptance, and commitment. Yet, it can bring joy, fulfillment, and meaning to our lives. A tremendous biblical reference point for shared values concerning love is I Corinthians 13:1.

"If I speak in the tongues of men or of angels, but do not have love, I am only a resounding gong or a clanging cymbal. 2 If I have the gift of prophecy and can fathom all mysteries and all knowledge, and if I have a faith that can move mountains, but do not have love, I am nothing. 3 If I give all I possess to the poor and give over my body to hardship that I may boast, but do not have love, I gain nothing. 4Love is patient, love is kind. It does not envy, it does not boast, it is not proud. 5 It does not dishonor others, it is not self-seeking, it is not easily angered, it keeps no record of wrongs. 6 Love does not delight in evil but rejoices with the truth. 7 It always protects, always trusts, always hopes, always perseveres. 8 Love never fails. But where there are prophecies, they will cease; where there are tongues, they

will be stilled; where there is knowledge, it will pass away. 9 For we know in part, and we prophesy in part, 10but when completeness comes, what is in part disappears. 11 When I was a child, I talked like a child, I thought like a child, I reasoned like a child. When I became a man, I put the ways of childhood behind me. 12 For now we see only a reflection as in a mirror; then we shall see face to face. Now I know in part; then I shall know fully, even as I am fully known.

13 And now these three remain: faith, hope and love. But the greatest of these is love."

2. CULTURAL

Marriage is a cultural institution that varies widely across different societies and cultures. However, here are some cultural aspects to consider concerning marriage:

- Marriage Customs: Different cultures have customs and traditions surrounding the marriage, such as wedding ceremonies, engagement rituals, and gift-giving practices. Understanding and respecting these customs when planning a wedding or getting married in a different culture is essential.

- Family Dynamics: In many cultures, marriage involves two individuals and their families. Family dynamics can impact the decision to get married, the choice of partner, and the extended family's level of involvement and support.
- Religion: Religion can play a significant role in marriage, from the choice of partner to the wedding ceremony and family traditions. It's important to consider how religion may impact the decision to get married and how it may shape the expectations and responsibilities within the marriage.
- Legal Aspects: The legal aspects of marriage can vary widely across cultures, from the age of consent to the rights and responsibilities of the partners. Understanding marriage's legal requirements and implications in your culture and location is essential.

Social Expectations: Cultural expectations surrounding marriage can impact the decision to get married, the choice of partner, and the expectations for the relationship. It's important to consider how social expectations may influence your decision to get married and how they may shape your relationship with your partner.

Overall, cultural aspects play a significant role in marriage, from customs and traditions to family dynamics, gender roles, religion, legal aspects, and social expectations. Therefore, it's essential to consider these cultural factors when deciding to get married and navigating the challenges and opportunities within the marriage.

3. EMOTIONAL

Marriage is a significant decision that can bring both joy and challenges. Therefore, it is essential to consider various emotional aspects before taking this step. Here are some of the vital emotional factors to consider before marriage:

- Compatibility: It is essential to assess your compatibility with your partner regarding emotional, physical, and intellectual compatibility. Compatibility can affect how you communicate, resolve conflicts, and make decisions together.
- Communication: Communication is the foundation of any healthy relationship. Before getting

married, it is essential to understand how well you communicate with your partner and how you both express your feelings and needs.

- Trust: Trust is a crucial factor in any relationship, and building trust with your partner before getting married is vital. Trust is built over time, requiring open communication, honesty, and commitment.
- Shared Values: Shared values can be important to consider before marriage, as they can affect how you make decisions and navigate challenges together. Understanding each other's values and beliefs can help you build a strong foundation for your relationship.
- Emotional Intelligence: Emotional intelligence is recognizing, understanding, and managing emotions effectively. It is essential to have emotional intelligence in a relationship to communicate effectively, empathize with your partner, and manage conflicts healthily.
- Future Goals: It is essential to consider your goals and aspirations and whether they align with your partner's goals. Having similar expected outcomes can help you work together as a team and support each other's dreams.

These emotional aspects can play a significant role in a successful marriage. Therefore, it is crucial to have open and honest conversations with your partner to ensure that you are both on the same page before getting married.

4. COMPANIONSHIP

Companionship is an essential aspect of a successful marriage. Therefore, couples must understand what companionship means and how to cultivate it before marriage. Here are some things that teams should know about companionship before tying the knot:

- Companionship is more than physical attraction: While physical allure is essential to any romantic relationship, friendship goes beyond physical appearance. It involves a deep emotional connection, shared interests, and a mutual desire to spend time together.
- Communication is Critical: Good communication is essential for building companionship in a relationship. Couples should

be able to talk openly and honestly about their feelings, needs, and expectations.

- Quality time matters: Spending quality time together is crucial for building companionship. Couples should make an effort to prioritize time for each other, whether it's going on dates, doing activities together, or just talking and sharing their thoughts and feelings.
- Shared interests can strengthen companionship: Couples with common interests and hobbies tend to have a more vital friendship. Finding activities that both partners enjoy and doing them together can help to deepen the emotional connection and create shared memories.
- Companionship requires effort and commitment: Building and maintaining friendship in a relationship takes effort and commitment from both partners. It requires a willingness to listen, compromise, and make time for each other, even when life gets busy.
- Companionship can evolve over time: As couples grow and change, their friendship may develop into new dynamics. It's essential to be

open to new experiences and be willing to adapt to each other's changing needs and interests.

Understanding these aspects of companionship can help. Couples build a strong foundation for their relationship and
lay the groundwork for a happy and fulfilling marriage.

5. RELIGIOUS BELIEFS

Understanding and respecting each other's religious beliefs is essential for building a solid and fulfilling Christian marriage. Here are some things that Christian couples should know about each other's religious beliefs before getting married:

- Shared faith: Understanding and sharing each other's faith before marriage is essential. A shared faith can help couples build a strong foundation for their relationship and provide a common understanding of values and beliefs.
- Denominational differences: Even within the Christian faith, there can be differences in denominations, traditions, and beliefs. Couples

need to discuss and understand each other's denominational differences and find ways to respect and accommodate these differences in their relationship.

- Personal beliefs and values: Couples should discuss their beliefs and values and how they align with their faith. This includes prayer, church attendance, tithing, and other spiritual practices.
- Family traditions and expectations: It is essential to discuss and understand each other's family traditions and expectations around faith. This can include holidays, family gatherings, and religious practices.
- How to handle conflicts: Couples need to discuss and agree on handling disputes that may arise around their faith. This can include topics such as raising children in the faith, disagreements about religious practices, and handling disagreements with family members.
- Support system: Christian couples should also discuss and understand each other's support systems within their faith community. This can

include church groups, Bible studies, and other spiritual communities.

Understanding and respecting each other's religious beliefs is essential for building a solid and fulfilling marriage for Christian couples. Couples can lay the foundation for a happy and supportive lifelong partnership by discussing these critical topics before marriage.

6. FINANCIAL STABILITY

Financial stability is an essential factor to consider before getting married. It can significantly impact the quality and longevity of a marriage. Here are some reasons why economic stability is critical to a marriage:

- Avoiding financial stress: Financial stress is one of the leading causes of relationship problems and divorce. By having a stable financial foundation, couples can avoid the stress and anxiety of economic instability.

- Planning for the Future: Financial stability enables couples to prepare for their future together, such as saving for a house, starting a family, or taking vacations. It helps them to set goals and work towards them as a team.
- Shared responsibility: Marriage is a partnership, and financial stability requires shared responsibility. Couples should discuss their financial goals, create a budget, and work together to manage their finances effectively.
- Building trust: Financial stability can also build trust in a relationship. When both partners are financially responsible and transparent with their finances, it can strengthen their emotional connection and faith.
- Resolving conflicts: Financial disagreements can be a significant source of conflict in a marriage. Couples can avoid or better manage financial disputes with a stable financial foundation.
- Security and stability: Financial stability can provide security and stability in a marriage. It allows couples to feel more confident about their

future and focus on other aspects of their relationship.

Overall, financial stability is an essential aspect of a successful marriage. It requires open communication, shared responsibility, and planning for the future. By discussing and understanding each other's financial situation before getting married, couples can set themselves up for a happier and more secure future together.

7. PERSONAL FULFILLMENT

Personal fulfillment is a vital aspect of a successful and fulfilling marriage. When both partners feel fulfilled and satisfied with their lives and relationship, it can lead to a more meaningful and rewarding partnership. Here are some reasons why personal fulfillment is significant in a marriage:

- Happiness and well-being: Personal fulfillment can lead to greater happiness and well-being in both partners. When individuals are fulfilled personally, it can translate to a more positive and joyful relationship.

- Emotional connection: Personal fulfillment can also lead to a stronger passionate relationship between partners. When both partners are fulfilled and satisfied, they are more likely to feel connected and engaged with each other.
- Shared interests and goals: Personal fulfillment can also involve pursuing shared interests and goals as a couple. When both partners are passionate about similar things, it can deepen the emotional connection and create shared experiences.
- Support and encouragement: When both partners feel fulfilled in their personal lives, they are better equipped to support and encourage each other. This can lead to a more positive and supportive relationship.
- Avoiding resentment: When one partner feels unfulfilled or dissatisfied in their personal life, it can lead to resentment towards their partner. By prioritizing personal fulfillment, couples can avoid this source of conflict in their relationship.

- Long-term satisfaction: Personal fulfillment can also lead to long-term happiness in a marriage. When both partners are fulfilled and satisfied with their lives and their relationship, it can lead to a more meaningful and rewarding partnership.

Overall, personal fulfillment is crucial to a successful and fulfilling marriage. Couples can create a more positive, meaningful, and satisfying partnership by prioritizing personal satisfaction and supporting each other's goals and interests.

8. A DESIRE TO START A FAMILY

Before marriage, couples must have open and honest conversations about their desire to start a family. Here are some things that everyone needs to know about their partner's desire to start a family before getting married:

- Timing: Couples should discuss when they want to start a family, including age, career goals, and financial stability. Understanding each other's timelines and expectations for starting a family is essential.

- Size of the family: Couples should also discuss their expectations for their family size. This can involve discussing the number of children they want and the spacing between them.
- Parenting styles: It is important to discuss parenting styles and approaches to discipline before starting a family. This can involve discussing how to handle challenging behavior, the role of each parent in parenting, and balancing work and family life.
- Financial planning: Couples should also discuss their financial plans and expectations for starting a family. This can include childcare costs, medical expenses, and the impact on their career goals.
- Support system: Understanding each other's support systems and how they will be involved in starting and raising a family is essential. This can include discussing the role of extended family members, friends, and other support networks.

- Health considerations: Couples should also discuss any health considerations affecting their ability to start a family, such as fertility issues, genetic conditions, or other health concerns.

By having open and honest conversations about their desire to start a family, couples can ensure they are on the same page and have a solid plan for creating and raising a family. This can lead to a more positive, supportive, and fulfilling family life.

Of course, there is no universal checklist for being ready for marriage. Instead, it is a personal decision that depends on many factors, such as emotional maturity, financial stability, and readiness for commitment.

However, some signs that a person may be ready for marriage include feeling emotionally secure and compatible with their partner, having open communication, and sharing similar values and goals for the future.

Ultimately, reflecting on one's feelings and aspirations is essential before committing.

Chapter 2

WIVES TO BE
The Biblically Defined Purpose of a Wife

The Bible clearly outlines a specific purpose for a wife. It also provides guidance on how a wife should relate to her husband and how a husband should treat his wife.

Ephesians 5:22-33, it says: *"Wives, submit yourselves to your own husbands as you do to the Lord. For the husband is the head of the wife as Christ is the head of the church, his body, of which he is the Savior. Now as the church submits to Christ, so also wives should submit to their husbands in everything. Husbands, love your wives, just as Christ loved the church and gave himself up for her to make her holy, cleansing her by the washing with water through the word, and to present her to himself as a radiant church, without stain or wrinkle or any other blemish, but holy and blameless. In this same way, husbands ought to love their wives as their own bodies. He who loves his wife loves himself. After all, no one ever hated their own body, but they feed and care for their body, just as Christ does the church— for we are members of his body. "For this reason, a man will leave his father and mother and be united to his wife, and the two will become one flesh." This is a profound mystery—but I am talking about Christ and the church. However, each one of you also must love his wife as he loves himself, and the wife must respect her husband."*

These passages teach that a husband should love his wife sacrificially and selflessly, as Christ loved the church. It also teaches that a wife should submit to her husband's leadership, as the church is called to submit to Christ. However, it is essential to note that these roles are not meant to be oppressive or hierarchical. Still, rather they are intended to reflect the love and sacrifice of Christ.

According to the Bible, God created woman from the rib of man. Genesis 2:21-22, it says: *"So the Lord God caused the man to fall into a deep sleep; and while he was sleeping, he took one of the man's ribs and then closed up the place with flesh. Then the Lord God made a woman from the rib he had taken out of the man, and he brought her to the man."*

This passage suggests that women are created as companions for men. To be by his side and to help him. Genesis 1:27, it says: *"So God created mankind in his own image, in the image of God he created them; male and female he created them."* This suggests that men and women are created in God's image and equal in worth and dignity.

Genesis 2:18, it says: "The Lord God said, 'It is not good for the man to be alone. I will make a helper suitable for him.'" This passage suggests that woman was created to be a helper for a man. The word "helper" in this passage comes from the Hebrew word "ezer," which can also be translated as "companion," "assistant," or "ally."

The concept of a helper or companion is often understood in a partnership, where both individuals contribute their unique skills, strengths, and perspectives to achieve common goals. In this sense, a woman can be a helpmate to her husband by supporting him, encouraging him, and working alongside him in their shared endeavors.

A helpmate does not imply inferiority or subordination. On the contrary, mutuality and interdependence are essential in healthy relationships. Both men and women are created in God's image and are equal in worth and dignity.

A woman is a female human being. The term "woman" refers to the adult female of the species, distinct from a girl or a man. Women have unique physical characteristics and experiences often associated with being female, including the ability to bear children and the presence of female reproductive organs.

However, it is crucial to recognize that gender is a complex and multifaceted aspect of a person's identity. Each woman is unique and has her own experiences, characteristics, and personality. Therefore, defining a person based on a limited set of characteristics or traits could be more productive and helpful. Instead, it is vital to recognize and respect the individuality and complexity of each person.

Specific characteristics and experiences are uniquely associated with being female, such as the ability to bear children and the presence of specific reproductive organs. However, it is essential to recognize that each woman is unique and has her own experiences, characteristics, and personality.

Here are a few key points that may help women feel good about having babies:

1. The experience of pregnancy and childbirth can be a significant and transformative experience for many women.
2. Having a baby can be a source of joy and fulfillment, allowing women to nurture and care for a new life.
3. Parenting can be a rewarding and challenging experience that allows women to grow and develop as individuals.
4. Many women find a sense of purpose and connection through motherhood, as it allows them to contribute to the next generation and positively impact the world.
5. Having a baby can also strengthen relationships and create new bonds within families and communities.

It is essential to recognize that every woman's experience of pregnancy and motherhood is unique and that it is normal to have a range of emotions during this time. It is also essential to seek support and guidance and prioritize self-care to maintain physical and emotional well-being.

Being a wife is a multifaceted role that involves a wide range of responsibilities and expectations. However, here are a few things involved in being a wife:

1. Building and maintaining a solid and supportive relationship with your spouse. This may involve communication, compromise, and a commitment to working together to achieve common goals.
2. Managing household responsibilities and tasks, such as cooking, cleaning, and caring for children or dependents.
3. Providing emotional support and encouragement for your spouse.
4. Being a partner and companion to your spouse through the ups and downs of life.
5. Being open to compromise and finding ways to work together to meet the needs and goals of both partners.

It is essential to recognize that being a wife means different things to different people and that a wife's specific roles and responsibilities may vary depending on individual circumstances and the needs of the relationship. It is also important to remember that a healthy and fulfilling relationship requires effort and commitment from both partners.

The Old Testament does contain passages that provide guidance on the roles and responsibilities of a wife. For example, Proverbs 31 describes a virtuous wife as hardworking, wise, and compassionate. It says:

"A wife of noble character who can find? She is worth far more than rubies. Her husband has complete confidence in her and lacks nothing of value. She brings him good, not harm, all the days of her life. She selects wool and flax and works with eager hands. She is like the merchant ships, bringing her food from afar. She gets up while it is still dark; she provides food for her family and portions for her female servants. She considers a field and buys it; out of her earnings, she plants a vineyard. She sets about her work vigorously; her arms are strong for her tasks. She sees that her trading is profitable, and her lamp does not go out at night. In her hand, she holds the distaff and grasps the spindle with her fingers. She opens her arms to the poor and extends her hands to the needy. When it snows, she has no fear for her household; all of them are clothed in scarlet. She makes coverings for her bed; she is

clothed in fine linen and purple. Her husband is respected at the city gate, where he takes his seat among the elders of the land. She makes linen garments and sells them and supplies the merchants with sashes. She is clothed in fine linen and purple and her husband is respected at the city gate, where he takes his seat among the elders of the land. She is clothed in fine linen and purple and her husband is respected at the city gate, where he takes his seat among the elders of the land. She is clothed in fine linen and purple and her husband is respected at the city gate, where he takes his seat among the elders of the land. She is clothed in fine linen and purple and her husband is respected at the city gate, where he takes his seat among the elders of the land."

This passage describes a wife who is diligent, resourceful, and supportive of her husband and her household. It also emphasizes her kindness and generosity towards others.

It is important to note that the roles and responsibilities of a wife may vary depending on individual circumstances and cultural context. However, it is also essential to recognize that the Bible teaches that men and women are equal in worth and dignity and that healthy relationships are characterized by mutual respect and love.

Chapter 3

THE HATS HUSBANDS WEAR
The Interchanging Duties of Being a Spouse

In marriage, both husbands and wives wear many different hats, taking on various roles and responsibilities as they navigate the ups and downs of life together. While both partners play essential roles in the marriage, the Bible specializes in the husband's role as the head of the household. Here are some of the different hats that husbands and wives wear in marriage:

Hats that Husbands Wear:

- Provider - Husbands are responsible for providing for their families, both financially and emotionally. This means working to support the family while being emotionally present and supportive of their spouse and children.
- Spiritual Leader - As mentioned earlier, husbands are called spiritual leaders in their homes, helping their wives grow in their faith and leading by example in living a godly life.
- Protector - Husbands are called to protect their families, both physically and emotionally. This means being a source of strength and security for their wives and children and taking steps to keep them safe from harm.

- Communicator - Husbands are called to be effective communicators with their wives and children. This means listening well, expressing their thoughts and feelings clearly, and working to resolve conflicts constructively and lovingly.
- Lover - Husbands are called to be loving and attentive to their wives, both physically and emotionally. This means making time for intimacy and affection and showing their love in everyday acts of kindness and service.

Hats that Wives Wear:
- Supporter - Wives are called to support their husbands, both emotionally and practically. This means being a source of encouragement, helping their husbands achieve their goals, and being a partner in their shared endeavors.
- Homemaker - Wives are often responsible for creating a comfortable and welcoming home environment, taking care of household tasks, and nurturing their children.
- Communicator - Wives are called to be effective communicators with their husbands and children.

This means listening well, expressing their thoughts and feelings clearly, and working to resolve conflicts constructively and lovingly.
- Lover - Wives are called to be loving and attentive to their husbands, both physically and emotionally. This means making time for intimacy and affection and showing their love in everyday acts of kindness and service.
- Spiritual Partner - Wives are called to be spiritual partners with their husbands, helping them grow in their faith and supporting them in their spiritual journey.

Both husbands and wives wear many different hats in marriage, taking on various roles and responsibilities as they work together to build a strong, healthy, and fulfilling relationship. While both partners play essential roles in the marriage, the Bible specializes in the husband's role as the head of the household. By fulfilling these roles with love, compassion, and devotion, husbands and wives can create a solid and lasting bond that honors God and brings joy and fulfillment to both partners.

As Christians, we believe marriage is a sacred covenant established by God between a man and a woman. In Ephesians 5:25-33, the Apostle Paul outlines the roles of husbands and wives in marriage. In this passage, Paul teaches that husbands have a specific purpose within the marriage.

The husband is to love his wife as Christ loved the church.

A husband's first and most important purpose is to love his wife as Christ loved the church. This means that the husband is to be self-sacrificing, putting the needs and well-being of his wife above his own. Just as Christ gave Himself up for the church, the husband is to give himself up for his wife.

The husband is to sanctify his wife.

In Ephesians 5:26-27, Paul writes that husbands are to sanctify their wives, cleansing them with the word of God. This means that the husband is to be a spiritual leader in the home, leading his wife in the ways of God and helping her grow in her faith.

The husband is to present his wife as holy and blameless.

Paul continues in Ephesians 5:27, writing that husbands are to present their wives as holy and blameless. This means that the husband is to cherish and care for his wife, protecting her from harm and helping her to grow and thrive in all areas of her life.

The husband is to love his wife as his own body.

In Ephesians 5:28-29, Paul writes that husbands are to love their wives as their bodies, nourishing and cherishing them just as Christ does the church. This means that the husband is to care for his wife's physical needs, as well as her emotional and spiritual needs.

The husband is to leave his parents and cleave to his wife.

In Genesis 2:24, we read that a man shall leave his father and mother and be joined to his wife, who shall become one flesh. This means that the husband is to prioritize his relationship with his wife above all others, including his relationship with his parents.

The husband is to be a servant-leader.

In Matthew 20:26-28, Jesus teaches that those who want to be great must be servants of all. This means that the husband is to be a servant-leader, putting his wife's needs above his own and leading by example in all areas of his life.

The purpose of a husband in marriage is to love and serve his wife as Christ loved and served the church. This means being a spiritual leader, caring for his wife's physical and emotional needs, prioritizing his relationship with his wife above all others, and being a servant-leader in all areas of his life. By fulfilling these purposes, the husband can help create a strong, healthy, and fulfilling marriage that honors God and brings joy and fulfillment to both partners.

THE BENEFITS OF BEING A HUSBAND

Marriage is a beautiful institution ordained by God. It is a union between two people committed to loving and caring for each other for the rest of their lives. While both partners bring unique qualities and gifts to the relationship, there are many benefits to having a man in marriage.

One of the main benefits of having a man in marriage is his ability to provide. In many cultures and societies, men are seen as the primary breadwinners and providers for their families. This is not to say that women cannot also provide for their families, but having a man in marriage often means having a willing partner who can work hard to support his family financially.

Another benefit of having a man in marriage is his strength and protection. Men are often physically stronger than women, making them better equipped to protect their families from harm. This does not mean that women cannot also be strong and protective, but having a man in marriage can provide his family an additional layer of security and safety.

Men also bring a unique perspective and approach to problem-solving in marriage. They tend to be more direct and logical in their thinking, which can be helpful in situations where quick decisions need to be made. This can complement women's more nurturing and intuitive approach to the relationship.

In addition, having a man in marriage can provide emotional support and stability. Men are often taught from a young age to be strong and stoic. Still, in a loving and trusting relationship, they can open up emotionally and be vulnerable with their partner. This can create a deeper level of intimacy and connection in the relationship.

Finally, having a man in marriage can also provide a positive role model for children. Boys can look up to their fathers as examples of what it means to be a man, and girls can learn what to expect from a loving and respectful relationship with a man.

Of course, not all men are the same, and not all will bring these qualities to a marriage. It is important to remember that every individual is unique, and every relationship is different. However, when a man is committed to loving and caring for his partner and family, there are many benefits to having him in marriage.

Being a functional man in marriage allows you to provide financial support, physical protection, a unique perspective and problem-solving approach, emotional support and stability, and a positive role model for children. When both partners work together and support each other in their different roles, they can create a solid and fulfilling marriage that honors God and brings joy and fulfillment to both partners.

Chapter 4

PREPARING FOR MARRIAGE
Steps to Take Prior to Meeting the One

You are a whole person, not half, which means you must learn to be confident and secure with yourself. Many assume that since the Bible says upon marriage, "the two become one," they reduce themselves and minimize their identity. Instead, you should start your relationship with a sense of self-worth, identity, and wholeness. No sound-minded person wants a broken version of you.

Broken individuals become closed off to what God has in store for them. However, you will become content after taking the proper steps of letting go of your baggage and becoming whole.

Once you are whole, you can enter a fully functional relationship where a husband and wife become one. The process occurs when you spend quality time engaging in conversations that intertwine your passions. The connection will diminish when you are not whole and happy with yourself. Don't seek after relationships to make you happy - that's what we call "looking for love in all the wrong places."

Looking for love in all the wrong places means seeking a romantic relationship or love in ways unlikely to lead to a positive outcome. This phrase typically refers to situations where someone repeatedly pursues romantic relationships or partners who are not well-suited for them or who may be unavailable, leading to frustration, disappointment, and potentially harmful consequences.

For example, someone might be looking for love in all the wrong places if they consistently pursue romantic relationships with people who are emotionally unavailable or who treat them poorly. Yet, they may continue to invest time and energy into these relationships, even when it is clear that they are not healthy or fulfilling.

Another example might be someone looking for love in all the wrong places by using dating apps or online platforms in a way that leads to disappointment and frustration. They may be swiping endlessly, hoping to find the perfect match, but end up dating people who are not a good fit for them.
Essentially, looking for love in all the wrong places means seeking a romantic relationship in ways that are not healthy, productive, or likely to lead to a positive outcome. Therefore, it's essential to take a step back, reflect on why you may be drawn to specific partners or dating behaviors, and consider how to change your approach to

increase your chances of finding a healthy, fulfilling relationship.

There are many reasons why people may look for happiness in relationships rather than from within themselves. One of the most common reasons is that society often emphasizes finding a partner as the key to happiness and fulfillment. Movies, TV shows, and popular culture often portray the idea that finding a soulmate or partner is the goal in life, which can lead people to believe that happiness depends on being in a relationship.

Additionally, some individuals may feel a sense of loneliness or emptiness that they believe can be filled by a romantic partner. They may consider having someone to share their life with will bring them joy, companionship, and a sense of purpose.

Another reason why people may look for happiness in relationships because they may have yet to learn to cultivate happiness and fulfillment from within themselves. They may have yet to develop a strong self-awareness, making it difficult to feel content and satisfied with their company.

It's important to note that seeking happiness in a relationship is okay. Humans are social creatures, and relationships can provide connection, love, and support to enhance our lives. However, it's essential to recognize that true happiness and fulfillment come from within and seeking it solely from a relationship can put undue pressure on the other person and ultimately lead to disappointment and dissatisfaction. Instead, learning to cultivate happiness from within can lead to a more fulfilling and satisfying life, both within and outside of a relationship.

Working On You

To work on self means engaging in a deliberate and ongoing process of personal growth and development, which involves taking responsibility for one's thoughts, feelings, and behaviors and making conscious efforts to improve them. This can involve a range of practices, such as self-reflection, self-awareness, self-compassion, and self-improvement, to enhance one's overall well-being and life satisfaction.

Good character is a great asset for people seeking to get married because it forms the foundation of a healthy and fulfilling relationship. When two people with good character traits come together in a marriage, they are more likely to create a strong, respectful, and loving partnership that can withstand the ups and downs of life.

Here are a few reasons why a good character is vital in a marriage:

1. Trust: Good character traits like honesty, integrity, and loyalty are essential for building relationships and trust. When both partners exhibit these traits, they can trust each other completely, which is crucial for building a solid foundation for the marriage.
2. Respect: Good character traits like kindness, empathy, and respect for others are essential for maintaining a healthy and respectful relationship. When both partners treat each other respectfully and kindly, they are more likely to have a positive and fulfilling marriage.
3. Communication: Good character traits like openness, honesty, and empathy are essential for effective communication in a marriage. When both partners are willing to communicate openly and honestly with each other, they can work through challenges and conflicts more effectively.

4. Support: Good character traits like compassion, generosity, and selflessness are essential for supporting and encouraging each other in a marriage. When both partners are willing to help each other through difficult times, they can strengthen their relationship and deepen their love for each other.

Good character is a great asset for people seeking marriage because it creates a strong foundation for a healthy, loving, and fulfilling relationship. When both partners exhibit good character traits, they can build a relationship built on trust, respect, communication, and support, leading to a lifetime of happiness and fulfillment.

So, start by working on your character before focusing on others. Trying to enter a relationship with trust issues within yourself. Ask yourself the following question and write down your answers:

- Who are you?
- Are You Reliable?
- Are You Trustworthy?
- Are You an honest person?
- What are you bringing to the table?

- Have you put your attitude in check?

Sometimes you also need to ask yourself these questions about your character. Avoid justifying your actions with unwanted excuses by writing down crucial components that describe the current version of yourself.

- This Is the Way God Made Me
- I Am Good How I Am
- Nasty Attitudes
- Easily Angered
- Except Me for Who I Am

When your attitude changes with the weather, that is likely to harm your relationship. To enter a relationship, you must know that these things matter.

The Parent Test

As it relates to the relationships with your mother and father, are you following what the word says in Ephesians 6:2-3, *"Honor your father and mother,"* which is the first commandment with promise: *"that it may be well with you, and you may live long on the earth."*

You want to look at how your person of interest treats their mother or father. What kind of relationship do they have, and will you be okay with their behavior when that treatment comes to you?

From a female perspective, when men demonstrate love for their mothers, they will show a similar love toward their wives. So how people treat their parents is a phenomenal test determining how they'll treat you.

Get A Life

How many people can honestly say that they have a life? Falling into the thirst trap of needing to be with someone can be crippling. Both men and women should learn how to do things alone, such as:

- Traveling
- Hobbies
- Going To Dinner
- Cook and Clean
- Going To the Movies
- Pay Bills

Maintain a healthy relationship with friends, do what you want and like, and not wait for someone else to make things happen.

Having good and healthy relationships with friends is essential to your well-being. So, taking that emotional and mental break and spending time with your girlfriends or male friends can help strengthen your relationship.

Having space and giving each other space is also a part of maintaining and having a healthy relationship.

Spending Time Alone

Spending time alone can be a unique experience for everyone on an individual level. Some people find it peaceful and rejuvenating, while others may feel bored or lonely.

It can offer a chance for reflection, self-discovery, and personal growth. Also, balancing time alone and socializing with others is admirable.

Some people love spending time alone, but most often, these people are introverts - the rest of us must learn how.

There is a joke that says, "I love me some me." It's an expression some people use as self-encouragement. Being alone means, you love the space and place you occupy. However, you need to be with yourself and learn to like who you are before you expect someone else to love you for a lifetime.

Unfortunately, some people despise the idea of being alone. It is a common misconception that all extroverts enjoy being around people all the time and dislike being alone. Extraversion refers to a person's preference for social interaction and stimulation, but this does not necessarily mean they cannot enjoy or appreciate solitude.

However, being alone may be uncomfortable or even anxiety-inducing for some extroverts, as they derive their energy and emotional fulfillment from social interaction. As a result, they may feel bored, restless, or lonely without the stimulation of others. They may crave constant social contact to feel energized and happy.

Furthermore, some individuals may feel pressure to conform to social expectations that extraverts should always be outgoing and friendly, making them feel guilty or ashamed when they crave alone time or do not enjoy socializing as much as others.

Overall, it is essential to recognize that extraversion is a spectrum, and everyone has unique preferences and needs for social interaction and solitude.
Many people get into a relationship because they dislike being alone or lonely. But unfortunately, that mentality is a recipe for disaster which could cause you to settle for anything, all in the name of loneliness.

Start Having Standards Now

From the beginning, you should have standards for the person you choose to share a relationship with. It helps ensure that you are in a healthy and fulfilling relationship.

What works for you may be different from what works for me. Your requirement may not be someone else's, but everyone should have standards. As a single person, we assemble a checklist of what we are looking for instead of letting God bring what we need to us.

Avoid putting so much on that checklist that it becomes complex. Instead, trust that God knows you and your needs better than you know yourself. So, when you are particular about your standards, don't be surprised when God gives you the desire of your heart.

Having standards, values, and morals will help you weed out the undesirables quickly.

They May Be the One

Be careful to avoid opening yourself up quickly and easily. When you find someone, you think might be the one, be cautious of what you share upfront because everything does not have to happen immediately.

Things you dealt with or went through in your past do not need to be discussed or shared at the beginning of a relationship. And some things are worth taking to your grave. They don't need to know everything. Likewise, some things you discover are null and void once in a long-term relationship or marriage.

According to Proverbs 18:22, *"He who finds a wife finds a good thing. And Obtains favor from the Lord."* So, when you find that potential one or that one finds you hiding in plain sight, you will find favor with God.

Refrain from taking your old stuff into your new relationship. And making sure that you are not holding the new relationship responsible for any past experiences. Many men and women have had something happen that they are unwilling to talk about with anyone but God, and that is where it will stay.

Suppose the trust in your relationship evolves to such conversations. In that case, you should not make that person feel guilty about their past. Transparent conversations make a person vulnerable. Don't attack their comfort by using their words as ammunition against them.

False Expectations of a Marriage

You must stop looking at television and social media for your relationship advice. It creates false expectations.

What you see on television is not reality but paid entertainment - even when labeled "Reality TV." But unfortunately, people seem to get tripped up with what they see on television or social media and start trying to redirect their relationships accordingly.

Firstly, they often portray idealized and unrealistic images of relationships, such as couples who seem in a constant state of bliss and never experience conflict or challenges. This can create the impression that a successful marriage is effortless and that any arising issues are a sign of failure or inadequacy.

Secondly, social media and TV can also create pressure to conform to certain relationship norms or standards, such as expensive weddings, frequent romantic gestures, or constant displays of affection. These expectations can be unrealistic or unattainable for many couples. Moreover, they can lead to feelings of disappointment or inadequacy if they are not met.

Finally, social media and TV can also create a sense of competition or comparison between couples, as individuals may feel pressure to keep up with the seemingly perfect relationships of others. This can lead to jealousy or insecurity and put unnecessary strain on new marriages.

Overall, individuals need to recognize that the images and expectations presented on social media and TV do not necessarily reflect reality and that every relationship is unique and will face challenges and ups and downs. Therefore, building a robust and supportive partnership with open communication and mutual respect is essential, rather than striving to meet unrealistic or unattainable expectations.

Social media and TV highlights false positives and illusions. Marriage is a choice and not an obligation. You could still have a healthy relationship with God and not be married.

If you are choosing to get married, make sure that you ask God if the person is his choice for you. Then, the Holy Spirit will guide you, whether the person was for you or not.

Are You on The Same Page

Make sure that you both are on the same page. Know that you are in tune with what you say to each other.

You must have conversations to know what the other is thinking. Do not allow your feelings to get in the way of those conversations.

Be prepared to talk things out and be okay when your significant other isn't ready for the next step. You must be okay with the outcome.

Suppose you are interested in someone and want to ensure you are on the same page. In that case, it is crucial to communicate openly and honestly with them. Here are some steps you can take:

- Clarify your feelings: Before conversing with the other person, take some time to reflect on your feelings and what you want from the relationship. Consider your expectations and boundaries and what you are looking for in a partner.
- Initiate a conversation: Once you clearly understand your feelings, initiate a conversation with the other person. This can be done in person or over the phone; choosing a time when you are relaxed and not distracted is essential.
- Share your thoughts and feelings: Be open and honest with the other person about your thoughts and feelings. Tell them what you are looking for in a relationship and your expectations. Ask them about their thoughts and feelings and be sure to actively listen to their response.

- Discuss expectations and boundaries: It is essential to discuss any expectations or limitations you have for the relationship. This can include topics such as communication, exclusivity, and future plans Be clear about what you are comfortable with and ask the other person to do the same.
- Follow up: After the conversation, following up and ensuring you are still on the same page is essential. Check in with the other person periodically to ensure you are both still comfortable with the direction of the relationship.

Overall, open and honest communication is vital to ensuring you are on the same page as someone you are interested in. By clarifying your own feelings, initiating a conversation, and discussing expectations and boundaries, you can build a strong foundation for a healthy and fulfilling relationship.

Compromise, Communicate, And Commit

If you are not ready to compromise, communicate, and commit, you are not prepared for marriage. Yet, all three factors are the foundation of every thriving marriage.

Men communicate differently than women, or at least they share a different priority regarding what needs to be discussed based on their opinions. Women want to discuss things with words, and many men share limited conversations about emotional matters.

Also, learning how to compromise is essential in a marriage. You can't always have it your way; that is not how it is in a marital relationship. Marriage is not an unhealthy fast-food drive-through where you can make orders and demands.

If you are not ready to communicate on the same level as each other, then you are not prepared for marriage. And as time changes in that marriage, so does the communication level. So, it would help if you stayed connected even when seasons are shifting.

Marriage is a beautiful union that God honors. However, committing to the relationship is no easy quest, so you must prepare before meeting that special person.

Chapter 5

RESTORING THE TEMPLE
Starting Over and Moving Forward

Once upon a time, a woman named Sarah had been married for ten years. Despite her efforts to save her marriage, she and her husband ultimately decided to get a divorce. Sarah felt lost and alone, unsure how to move forward and start rebuilding her life.

At first, Sarah was consumed by feelings of grief and despair. She struggled to get out of bed in the morning and often cried throughout the day. However, as time passed, Sarah realized she had an opportunity to start fresh and create a new life.

She began by focusing on her mental and physical health. Sarah started exercising regularly, eating healthier foods, and spending time outdoors in nature. She also began seeing a therapist to work through her emotions and process her feelings about the divorce.

As Sarah started to feel stronger and more grounded, she began to think about what she wanted her new life to look like. She set goals for herself, such as going back to school to pursue a degree in a field she was passionate about and traveling to places she had always wanted to visit.

Sarah also reconnected with old friends and made new ones. She joined a book club, volunteered at a local animal shelter, and started attending yoga classes. By getting involved in activities she enjoyed, Sarah began to build a sense of community and connection that had been missing from her life.

Over time, Sarah started to feel like she was surviving and thriving. She realized that although her marriage had ended, she had the power to create a fulfilling and happy life for herself. As a result, Sarah learned to let go of the past and focus on the present, knowing that the future was full of endless possibilities.

Ultimately, Sarah's journey of restoring her life after divorce wasn't easy, but it was worth it. She learned to value herself, embrace change, and create a life that brought her joy and fulfillment. Sarah's story is a reminder that although divorce can be a painful and challenging experience, Similar incidents have happened to countless men. Yet, it can also be a catalyst for growth and transformation.

When is Divorce the Only Option

People like to say that divorce is not an option in their relationship, and many people agree. However, it should be a person's mindset to force themselves to work out any problems they may encounter in their marriage. A marriage is based on vows.

Sometimes divorce is an option. Some situations might call for divorce, and sometimes it just happens. Christian counselors may have varying opinions on when divorce is acceptable among believers, as interpretations of scripture and beliefs can differ among individuals and denominations. However, some common reasons that Christian counselors may consider divorce acceptable among believers include the following:

1. Adultery or infidelity: According to many Christian counselors, adultery is considered biblical grounds for divorce (Matthew 5:32, 19:9). If one spouse has committed adultery, the other spouse may feel that divorce is necessary to protect their emotional and physical well-being.
2. Abuse: Physical, emotional, or sexual abuse in a marriage can be grounds for divorce in some

Christian counseling perspectives. Abuse violates the sacredness of marriage and endangers the safety and well-being of the victim.

3. Abandonment: Some Christian counselors may view abandonment as a legitimate reason for divorce (1 Corinthians 7:15). If one spouse leaves the marriage without any intention of returning, the other spouse may feel that divorce is necessary to move on with their life.
4. Irreconcilable differences: Some Christian counselors may view divorce as acceptable if the marriage is broken and both spouses have tried to reconcile.

It's important to note that divorce is generally not viewed as the ideal outcome in Christian counseling. Counselors often work with couples to try to save their marriage if possible. However, in some cases, divorce may be seen as a necessary option to protect the well-being of one or both spouses. If your marriage results in divorce, that does not mean there is no marriage in you. Restart your new relationship with the right resources and tools to ensure that it develops into a healthy marriage having nothing to do with the first.

The Next Relationship

Most people have been in a long or short-term relationship. But getting into any relationship, you never know how long it will last. Maintaining a long-term relationship requires a dedicated effort from both parties involved:

- Commitment
- Compromise
- Communication

Building a connection and showing interest can enhance the experience. But, whatever you do, avoid holding new people guilty for what someone did in your last relationship. Remember, you must take time to heal.

Both short and long-term relationships require the same ingredients. For example, most bakers know you must have all the ingredients in a pound cake to come out right, regardless of the cake size. With any relationship, no matter how short or long, you must approach it with the right ingredients.

Detoxing Everything You Have Heard and Seen

Detoxing from everything you have previously heard and seen can be difficult, but it's possible. Try meditation, mindfulness, and limiting your exposure to negative media. But it is also helpful to surround yourself with positive influences and engage in activities that bring you joy and relaxation.

It takes time and effort, but it's worth it for your mental and emotional well-being. But first, you should allow yourself to get rid of all the old stuff, such as:

- Hurt
- Pain
- Failed Marriage(s)
- Failed Relationship(s)
- Old Relationship Baggage

Most people compare their old experiences with what is going on in their new relationships. It's like having the ghost of relationships past hovering around, reminding you of what went wrong.

The hurt from past relationships is so intense on you that you are dragging around your old pain and can't get rid of it. It would help if you allowed yourself to get over all the old stuff.

Be transparent, truthful, and honest with yourself, and get over the stuff holding you back. You must have a clean slate and a pure heart before asking God to bless you with a new relationship.

Going into a new relationship with old stuff could taint the relationship and cause issues that could ruin an excellent relationship. Restore your temple by starting over and moving forward.

Index

Q&A SESSION
Singles Seminar 2023

Marriage provides many benefits, such as legal and financial protections, emotional support, companionship, and a sense of commitment and strength.

On a spiritual level, the connection in a marriage can vary based on individual beliefs. Still, generally, it involves a deep understanding and connection with one partner.

When asked, "Why do you desire to be married?" Many participants agreed on the following:

- Companionship
- Partnership
- Someone To Grow With

Answers also involve having someone who shares your values, beliefs, and practices. Everyone hopes for a person who will enhance the relationship and promote unity and purpose.

The questions did not have age limits attached which got responses from adults mature as age 70. That shows that marriage is desired at any age if you are receptive. Most people want a life partner. Someone to spend time with, share experiences with, or provide emotional support and friendship.

Most singles seek someone to grow with who will work together to make life decisions, share responsibilities, communicate openly, and solve problems. In addition, quality singles respect their significant other's opinions.

Our question and answer (Q&A) sessions are highly beneficial for both my husband, Shawn, and I and our participants for several reasons:

- Engagement and Interaction: Q&A sessions allow for direct interaction and engagement between the presenter and the audience, which can increase audience participation and interest. This can lead to a more dynamic and engaging presentation overall.
- Clarification of Concepts: Q&A sessions allow the audience to ask questions and seek clarification on concepts they may have yet to understand fully during the presentation. This helps ensure that everyone has a better understanding of the material.

- Feedback: Q&A sessions also provide valuable feedback, allowing us to gauge the audience's understanding and identify areas where more explanation may be necessary.
- Knowledge Sharing: Q&A sessions can also facilitate knowledge-sharing among the audience members. Often, audience members will ask questions or share their experiences, which can be highly valuable and informative for everyone in the room.
- Personal Connection: Q&A sessions can build an intimate connection between the presenter and the audience. We can establish a rapport and build trust with our listeners by answering questions and engaging in a dialogue with the audience.

Overall, Q&A sessions are excellent for enhancing the effectiveness and impact of our presentations, fostering engagement and interaction, and promoting knowledge sharing and personal connection. The following questions and answers were presented during a 2023 singles seminar.

Questions & Answers

Question 1: How do you match each other's communication styles or sense the change in communication?

Response: Time will develop that sense of change in how you communicate. When you start to get more into talking to each other or the meat of the conversations with each other and learning about each other, you begin to go through all the seasons. People's attitudes change depending on the season, winter, spring, summer, or fall. You might need to pray and ask for help understanding the change in your relationship's communication during that time.

Question 2: Is there a time limit or requirement to dating someone before moving to the next step, marriage, or the "I Do's?"

Response: Within two years, you should know if that person is the one God has in store for you. If they are unsure, letting them go is also an option for you.

Question 3: Should the woman be looking for the man or waiting for that man to find them?

Response: She believes you should hide in plain sight. Be readily available.

Question 4: When a man meets that woman, they know from day one that they are "the one," is that true?

Response: She stated that sometimes that question is more of an old-school question from the older generation's thought pattern. Being safe and careful when going out dating in this day and time.

The question is from a different culture. We are now being limited by technology, such as online dating, to meet someone.

Question 5: From a female's perspective, when a man sees you and shows interest, is it ok to share and respond to that or reciprocate?

Response: She feels it is perfectly ok to respond back. How else would a man know that you are interested as well? At the beginning of a relationship, you don't know each other well enough, so communication, when dating, is necessary to get to know them spiritually, personally, and financially. Also, sometimes you want to see if you can afford to be with that person.

Question 6: In this new generation, trying to find someone who understands the dynamic of a two-parent household and you being a well-balanced person takes time to date.

Response: You must choose your community. This culture is complex. You know what you want, and you know your standards. Your community is the type of people you surround yourself with and is also what you will attract. Also, know your maturity level.

Question 7: Some people are set in their ways and still deal with their old stuff. Tired of meeting men with no stability with nothing to offer or bring to the table.

Response: It is all in the community you hang around. People live in the communities that they are more like. It is a difference in shopping at Big Lots than it is at SAKs. The quality is different. So, your level of style and conversation mimics what you are looking for in a partner and relationship. Also, don't overlook your potential person. Believe together, pray together.

Question 8: When that other person doesn't go to church or makes excuses not to go after being invited by you but will want you to go to the movies or someplace else. Those are red flags.

Response: It's your standards. People are willing to settle because they feel they will not have anyone. But by surrounding yourself with spiritually minded people who have that discernment to give you those signals that will alert you of possible mistakes, such as your pastor, in your dating choices. But you need to trust that God has the right person for you. And he knows what you need and your desires.

Question 9: Women will look outside of the church to find someone when that someone is right there in the church for them. Women say they want an alpha man, but when that man becomes the head and is ready to lead that woman, they are not prepared for that type of leadership in a relationship. Men have a kind of woman that they look for as well. Just because they love God doesn't mean they want their partner or spouse to be "holier than thou" or "too spiritual" all the time. Men want to be ministered to by their spouses and not just in a spiritual way. Women learn how to pray, while men learn how to prey. So, both coming together to hear each other can improve the relationship.

Response: Being too spiritual can cause you not to be datable. What type of conversation do you have? You need to know and be honest about your appetite in your relationship or potential relationship.

Question 10: How can you find balance being a church girl?

Response: You need that balance in a relationship. Dating and coming from a strict upbringing, you get to know your limits and learn to protect your spirituality. Be continent and not a needy type of person or "thirsty" for attention or having the urge to always be up under somebody all the time.

Question 11: What about meeting people who bring children into the relationship?

Response: It all comes down to communicating what you want and how each of you will raise that child or children. Contact with the other parent is also important.

Question 12: How do you deal with that one who is just a friend?

Response: Keep them as your friend, and do not let them occupy all of your time because you do not want that friend taking the space for whom God has for you. But also, that friend could be the one God has placed in your life.

Bishop Sean Bell's and Lady Faye's Final Words: Get yourself prepared for the place that person comes from. You must be careful. Being desperate, you open yourself up for things you are not prepared for. If you need a relationship so bad that you are willing to settle, be ready for the risks that come with it. Don't allow people into your life that will cause havoc. You need to be whole for your relationship. Take your time; why are you rushing? Get to know that person. Also, this may not be your season to be married, but it could be your season to be single.

Discuss these and many other questions with your soon-to-be husband or wife. Tackle one topic at a time, focusing on clear communication and understanding. Please don't make them feel pressured or cornered.

Champion honesty. Telling lies at this point will set your marriage on a foundation of mistrust. Instead, take things seriously and try to be as truthful as possible.

Use the opportunity to settle disagreements. When you enter a marriage, you should read from the same script on sex, money, children, and spousal responsibilities. Now may be the ideal time to compromise on things you view differently.

Set goals as you work through the questions with your future spouse. These could be budgetary goals and plans to repay debt, plans to move, get a new job, etc. Healthy relationship changes can lead to healthy marriages. Consider the following premarital questions to reduce arguments and disappointments on money, sex, marital roles, morals, values, and beliefs, conflict and issue resolution, and random life experiences:

Premarital Questions on Money:

1. Should we have joint or separate accounts? If not, what are the reasons for not being willing to share our assets? Is it trust or something else?
2. Should we have a prenuptial agreement? What reasons for this? Are you both being honest about your feelings as you enter the prenuptial?
3. What should our monthly budget look like? Do you know how to discuss your spending styles and relationship with money? Or are you afraid because you don't know how to face conflicts about this? Are you going to spend money and keep it secret and be in hiding?
4. Do you have an outstanding loan that I should know of? Do you have any debt that you are hiding?
5. Are you a saver or a spendthrift?

Premarital Questions on Sex

Great sex leads to happier marriages. Use these premarital counseling questions to learn how to satisfy your marriage partner:
1. How many times a week would you want to have sex?
2. What is your best sexual fantasy?
3. What is the most reliable way to achieve satisfaction?
4. What turns you off?
5. What gets you in the mood?
6. Do you have any fears about sex? Is there anything you are holding back?
7. Do you have feelings or thoughts about each other's sexual history before knowing them?
8. How do your trust issues show up in sex and your partner's interactions with the opposite sex?

Premarital Questions on Marital Roles

1. Find out how you will share responsibilities throughout your marriage and your expectations with each other? Be clear and specific about any responsibilities:

2. What role would you want to play in the marriage?
3. What role would you expect me to play?
4. How should we divide household chores?
5. Who will make the most significant decisions in the family?
6. What is the most challenging thing or issue about marriage?
7.

Premarital questions morals, values, and beliefs

Morals and values are the foundation of a healthy marriage. Here is how to be sure:

1. What are your religious/ beliefs about marriage? If you don't share the same faith or views on faith, you will undoubtedly have future struggles, especially in parenting. So be specific about what is important to you when practicing your faith etc.
2. What is considered infidelity to you? Discuss your definitions of an emotional affair, sexual integrity issues including physical and sexual affairs, and more. Be very honest and open here in terms of your expectations and fear.
3. In what ways should I show you that I love you?

4. What is your opinion on birth control?
5. What could make you lose your trust in me? Discuss red lights and green lights from each perspective. What will you not put up with, and what is okay with you.

Premarital questions on conflict and issue resolution

Every relationship encounters conflict. The below questions can help you know how to deal with issues when they arise later in marriage:

1. How do you handle arguments?
2. Would you want us to get couples therapy if we had problems?
3. Is career more important than family?
4. Do you discuss issues as they arise or deal with them later?
5. If I disagree with your family, which side would you choose?

Random life experience questions:

1. Do you like pets?

2. Would you be okay with me/you traveling alone with friends for a few weeks?
3. Are you willing to move if the need arises? How would we make that decision?
4. Would it bother you if I changed my religion in the future?
5. Do you have a health issue that I should know of?
6. How would you like to spend or how would we decide to spend our Holiday breaks with our parents or extended family? Discuss expectations here.

CONSIDER GETTING A MEDIATOR

A marriage counseling professional or premarital counselor can help the two of you to understand each other clearly. They can guide the discussion on critical matters and reduce conflict before marriage. They help you know each other much better, especially in areas that are not typically discussed until they otherwise arise.

Discuss the number of kids you want to have. Learn about your parenting style, like how you manage people. Are you someone who has a passive style or a direct style? All of this will show up in your parenting.

Another significant issue is the role of social media. Many marriages are falling apart because of emotional affairs that have begun from connecting to former high-school friends or buddies from the past. This especially occurs when the couple is highly stressed and feels disconnected and doesn't know how to meet each other's needs. Meeting an old flame or a friend over social media is destructive. Likewise, having inappropriate boundaries with co-workers disguised as being nice or friendly has led to affairs and pain.

Be sure to ask honest questions. Don't be afraid of asking hard questions. The more open and transparent you are, the better it will be for your marriage.

What Should You Cover in Premarital Counseling?

Regardless of which category you fit into, there are some topics you should expect to cover in premarital counseling. These topics include how you interact with each other's family and friends; money; sex; careers; parenting; how you will handle holidays and special events; and spirituality or faith.

What is Pre-Marriage Counseling?

People consider couples counseling a last-ditch effort to save a marriage rather than a healthy premarital activity. Pre-marriage counseling for couples is like offering a lifeboat before a couple sails to sea. The alternative is to wait for a couple to begin drowning and then toss them a floatation device at the last minute. The latter is far riskier. Prevention is critical, and it can mean the difference between a well-adjusted, healthy couple or a couple who is unprepared and blindsided by the challenges of marriage. The benefits of couples counseling before the wedding far outweigh the risks.

Why Couples Counseling Before Marriage Helps

There is a multitude of reasons why couples counseling before marriage works. Most of the reasons pre-marriage counseling is so important for couples before marriage is the opportunity to learn more about one another, build communication and problem-solving skills and identify any expectations that may be unspoken. Couples counseling before engagement and marriage also offers the benefit of an outside perspective on your relationship. When couples can openly share their thoughts and feelings in a safe, confidential environment, the counselor can share observations about the relationship and offer insight into areas that may need exploration. Seemingly minor issues that a couple may overlook during the early stages of a relationship are likely to become more significant problems as the relationship progresses. When couples participate in marriage counseling before marriage, it can help uncover these issues so that resolutions can be found before they become significant problems that may cause distancing. In a country where the divorce rate was at least 44.2% in 2022, it is wise for couples to thoroughly examine their relationships before tying the knot.

The Stigma of Couples Therapy Before Marriage

Unfortunately, couples counseling has a stigma that prevents many people from participating. Couples who invest time, effort, and energy into their relationship through pre-marriage counseling demonstrate a commitment that will likely pay off for years. When couples dare to examine their relationship and talk about their challenges and strengths, it brings them closer and can head off potential challenges in the future. Couples who fear premarital counseling may have underlying doubts that they are unwilling to examine, which may be a red flag for future issues. Some couples may worry that a counselor will take sides. Still, this fear should be allayed as therapists are trained to sit with clients objectively and assist couples in building greater understanding rather than casting blame. It is important to remember that counseling is a safe, confidential setting that can help couples connect and better understand one another's needs.

LOCAL CHURCH LEADER PREMARITAL ADVICE

The fact that a pastor has been married for over 20 years doesn't automatically make their advice trustworthy. However, it may indicate they have experience and knowledge in maintaining a successful marriage.

If a pastor has been married for over 20 years, they have likely faced many of the challenges of a long-term relationship and have learned how to overcome them. They may have also gained insights into effective communication, conflict resolution, and other essential aspects of a healthy marriage.

Ultimately, whether to trust the advice of a pastor who has been married for over 20 years will depend on several factors, including their reputation, values, and the nature of the advice they offer. Do your research before placing your premarital counseling in the hands of just anyone. It's always a good idea to consider multiple perspectives and to seek advice from trusted sources before making important decisions.

About the Author

MOTIVATIONAL SPEAKER
Creating a Culture of Healthy Marriages

God's grace embodies Lady A. Faye Bell - a woman of wisdom and inspiration. As a renowned speaker and lecturer, she has traveled extensively, captivating audiences at conferences and churches worldwide.

Raised in Bessemer City, N.C., Lady Bell, the cherished daughter of Roger and Gwendolyn Lomick, received her education from the esteemed Gaston County Public School before pursuing further studies at Gaston Community College. Her pursuit of knowledge continued as she obtained an AA Degree in Christian Leadership from Union Bible Theological Seminary, firmly believing in the invaluable combination of education and experience. Lady Bell attributes her spiritual growth and foundational values to the guidance of Pastors Robyn and Marilyn Gool. They are dedicated leaders of the Victory Christian Center in Charlotte, N.C., where she served in various ministry capacities.

For over a decade, Lady Bell has played a pivotal role in the Sheriff's Administrative Office of the City of Baltimore, positioning herself at the heart of city government.

Lady Bell possesses a divine anointing, enabling her to preach and teach the Word of God with grace and eloquence. Additionally, she has a thriving career as a lifestyle consultant, specializing in event planning and wedding coordination.

As the founder and owner of A. Faye Bell and Associates, she has established herself as an esteemed professional in her field. She is also a licensed life insurance agent.

Lady Bell co-authored her debut book, "Travailing Women - The Untold Story of a First Lady," a powerful source of encouragement and inspiration for women from all walks of life.

Lady Bell's ultimate partnership lies with her husband, Bishop Shawn L. Bell. Together, they are the visionary leaders of The Greater Paradise Christian Center, a vibrant and thriving urban church in Baltimore. Since its establishment in 2003, GPCC has profoundly impacted the Baltimore/Washington Metropolitan area. They effectively challenge members to embrace regional and global responsibilities. GPCC is a holistic center of hope, continually pioneering innovative approaches to ministry. The groundbreaking initiatives include adult day programs, youth-driven activities, Paradise Touch Apparel, a hair salon, and a 180-seat dining facility.

In addition, lady Bell fulfills her spiritual calling within the church as the Director of Women's Ministries. The Women of Paradise draw strength from their scriptural foundation in Ephesians 3:20, which affirms God's ability to exceed all expectations and work powerfully within them.

Beyond her professional accomplishments, Lady Bell finds the utmost fulfillment as a devoted wife, mother to Miss Olivia L. Bell, and a prayer warrior seeking to unfold every aspect of life and ministry predestined by God.

Made in the USA
Columbia, SC
14 May 2024